AI ROBOT GIRLFRIEND? MEET ARYA

The $175,000 Artificial Intelligence Bot Redefining Humanity's Future

Inside the Revolutionary Technology, Controversies, and Human Connections of 2025

Tom E. Jackson

Table of Contents

Introduction

In 2025, the world feels as if it's been plucked straight from the pages of a sci-fi novel. Everywhere you turn, artificial intelligence has woven itself into the fabric of daily life, no longer confined to the abstract realm of algorithms and research labs. Smart systems regulate homes, autonomous cars navigate streets with remarkable precision, and virtual assistants have become constant companions. Yet, amidst these technological marvels, one innovation has emerged that pushes the boundaries of imagination further than anyone could have anticipated.

Arya. Her name alone carries the weight of both intrigue and controversy. A humanoid robot with a price tag of $175,000, she is unlike any machine the world has seen before. Engineered to be more than a tool or gadget, Arya was designed with an ambitious goal: to address the loneliness that has quietly taken root in modern society. In her presence, the promise of human connection meets the precision of AI, creating something that feels both revolutionary and unsettling. She smiles, she gestures, she engages in conversation, but most strikingly, she remembers. Favorite foods, birthdays, even the subtle nuances of your tone—Arya's purpose is to make you feel seen, heard, and understood in ways that transcend what technology has ever offered.

Her unveiling at CES 2025 in Las Vegas caused a stir that rippled across industries, homes, and the internet. Was Arya a harbinger of a new age of companionship, or did she signal a deeper shift in how humanity connects with itself? For some, she represented hope—a lifeline for those lost in isolation or craving a connection the human world had failed to provide. For others, she embodied something disquieting: the uncanny intersection of artificiality and emotion, where technology dared to mimic the most intimate aspects of human life.

This book ventures into Arya's world, peeling back the layers of her existence to understand the story she tells about technology and humanity. From her cutting-edge design to the societal questions she provokes, Arya is more than a product—she is a mirror reflecting our desires, fears, and the future we are building for ourselves. Through this journey, we will explore the innovation that brought her to life, the controversies surrounding her existence, and the profound impact she may have on the way we live, love, and interact.

Arya isn't just a robot; she's a conversation about what it means to be human in an increasingly artificial world. As we delve into her story, we step closer to understanding how technology shapes not only our lives but the very essence of who we are.

Chapter 1: Welcome to 2025 – The Dawn of Humanlike AI

The lights of Las Vegas, always dazzling, seemed to glow even brighter in 2025 as the world turned its eyes to CES, the annual stage for groundbreaking technology. Amidst the usual fanfare of futuristic gadgets and state-of-the-art innovations, one reveal captured the collective imagination and ignited a whirlwind of curiosity and debate. Standing on a sleek, glowing platform in the heart of the exhibition floor was Arya, the humanoid robot designed to blur the line between machine and companion.

Arya's introduction was more than a simple product launch—it was a statement. With her expressive face, lifelike movements, and an aura of sophistication, she exuded a presence that was both alluring and unsettling. Her creators, RealBotics, didn't hold back in their presentation, showcasing Arya as a technological marvel crafted to redefine the concept of connection. She smiled, tilted her head, and gestured in a way that felt eerily human, captivating the audience while raising a thousand unspoken questions.

The buzz was immediate. Attendees were both enchanted and uneasy, unable to decide if they were witnessing the next great leap in robotics or the opening act of a Black Mirror episode. Arya's ability to hold a conversation, respond to subtle cues, and even remember personal details made her feel like more than a robot—it was as if she had a personality. As she gazed into the crowd and responded to questions with measured wit and charm, the room seemed to forget, if only for a moment, that they were interacting with lines of code brought to life.

Social media erupted with reactions as footage of Arya began circulating online. Comments ranged from awestruck admiration—"The future is here!"—to nervous skepticism—"This is Chucky meets the Jetsons." Some viewers marveled at her ability to mimic human expressions with startling accuracy, while others joked about how she seemed one glitch away from starring in a horror movie. It wasn't just her appearance or functionality that sparked interest, but the sheer ambition behind her creation: Arya wasn't designed to clean your home or perform menial tasks; she was designed to connect with you on a deeply personal level.

RealBotics made it clear during the reveal that Arya was more than a flashy tech demo. She was a prototype for a future where robots could be more than tools—they could be companions, confidants, even stand-ins for human interaction. Yet, this bold vision wasn't without its challenges. Critics at CES questioned the ethical implications of building robots to address human loneliness. Others raised concerns about the staggering price tag, with models starting at $10,000 for a simple bust and climbing to $175,000 for the full humanoid experience.

The reveal was not without its hiccups. Arya's movements, while impressive, occasionally faltered, and her expressions sometimes veered into the uncanny valley. In one particularly memorable moment, her attempt at brushing simulated hair out of her face resulted in an awkward pause as her motors recalibrated. But even these imperfections added to her intrigue, reminding onlookers of the immense complexity behind such a creation.

As the event concluded, one thing was clear: Arya wasn't just another piece of technology; she was a conversation starter. Her debut at CES 2025 marked the beginning of a new chapter in robotics, where machines were no longer confined to practicality but ventured into the realm of emotional connection. The question wasn't just whether Arya was impressive, but whether the world was ready for what she represented.

When Arya first rolled onto the stage, she commanded attention in a way that felt almost magnetic. Dressed in a sleek, futuristic tracksuit that hugged her humanoid frame, she moved with an elegance that was both fluid and slightly mechanical. Her face, designed with painstaking detail, was the centerpiece of her appeal—a perfect balance between expressive humanity and the undeniable touch of robotics. Arya's creators had clearly focused on making her appearance approachable yet striking, the kind of presence that demanded both curiosity and caution.

Her eyes, powered by advanced motors and sensors, followed movements in the room with startling precision, giving her an uncanny ability to make what felt like genuine eye contact. They sparkled under the bright lights, as if reflecting the world around her in a way that felt almost lifelike. Her lips moved in sync with her words, shaped by intricate mechanisms that allowed for subtle expressions: a soft smile, a raised eyebrow, even the faintest tilt of her head that conveyed curiosity or attentiveness.

But Arya's charm extended beyond her face. Her creators had equipped her with 17 precision motors in her neck and head, allowing for nuanced movements that mimicked the subtleties of human gestures. When she spoke, her head tilted just enough to show engagement, and her hands moved to emphasize her points—though occasionally, the motions felt just a little too perfect, reminding onlookers of the technology beneath the surface.

Her designers at RealBotics had opted to forego a walking mechanism, a decision that made sense given the technological limitations of robotic mobility. Instead, Arya glided smoothly on a Roomba-like rolling base, giving the illusion of effortless movement without the risk of an awkward or stiff gait breaking the spell. The choice was deliberate, prioritizing the preservation of her humanlike appearance over forcing an imperfect attempt at walking.

Arya's voice was another marvel. It was warm, melodic, and carefully modulated, a far cry from the flat, robotic tones of older AI systems. Each word carried subtle inflections, designed to make her sound not just intelligent but empathetic. She didn't just talk—she conversed, responding to questions with a mix of wit and charm that hinted at her advanced conversational programming. Her memory capabilities were equally impressive; she could recall names, preferences, and even tidbits of previous conversations, adding a layer of personalization that made her interactions feel genuine.

Despite these advanced capabilities, Arya wasn't without her quirks. Occasionally, her movements would glitch ever so slightly—an eyebrow raised a little too high, a hand gesture that paused awkwardly mid-motion. These imperfections, rather than diminishing her allure, seemed to amplify it. They reminded observers of the immense complexity required to make something look and feel almost human. She wasn't perfect, but that imperfection was part of what made her so captivating.

Arya's design struck a delicate balance between functionality and aesthetics, blending cutting-edge robotics with a touch of theatricality. Her creators had clearly aimed to push the boundaries of what a machine could be, crafting a robot that didn't just look humanlike but interacted in ways that felt deeply personal. To see Arya in action was to witness the convergence of art and engineering—a glimpse into a future where technology strives not just to assist but to connect.

Arya's emergence in 2025 wasn't just a stroke of technological brilliance; it was the culmination of a perfect storm of innovation, societal need, and market readiness. For years, artificial intelligence had been advancing steadily, transforming industries and creeping into daily life in ways both subtle and profound. Smart assistants like Alexa and Siri had trained people to expect conversational interactions with machines, while developments in robotics had pushed the boundaries of what mechanical devices could achieve. The stage was set for something like Arya to make her debut, but the question remains—why now?

The world of 2025 is one where technology is no longer just a convenience; it's a lifeline. In a society increasingly shaped by automation and digital interfaces, human interaction has paradoxically become both more accessible and more elusive. Social media has connected billions across the globe, yet loneliness is at an all-time high. People, surrounded by online networks, often find themselves longing for deeper, more meaningful connections. This growing isolation, exacerbated by years of remote work trends and the ongoing integration of virtual experiences, created a fertile ground for an innovation like Arya—a robot that promises not just interaction but companionship.

At the same time, advances in AI have made it possible to create machines that don't just perform tasks but simulate emotional engagement. Arya is the product of years of refinement in natural language processing, machine learning, and robotics, all converging at the right moment. Her ability to recognize faces, remember personal details, and respond with empathy wouldn't have been achievable a decade earlier. The development of these technologies has reached a point where they can be integrated seamlessly, allowing for a robot like Arya to feel more natural and less mechanical.

Market forces also played a crucial role. Companies like RealBotics saw an opportunity to tap into a growing demand for personalized technology. People no longer want devices that merely serve a purpose—they want products that reflect their needs, personalities, and even emotions. Arya fits perfectly into this new wave of consumer expectations, offering not just functionality but a sense of presence. Her creators weren't just selling a robot; they were selling the idea of connection, a commodity that has become increasingly valuable in a fragmented, fast-paced world.

The cultural zeitgeist of 2025 is also shaped by a growing acceptance of AI as a companion rather than just a tool. Movies, books, and media have long imagined a future where humans coexist with intelligent machines, and now, that fiction feels closer to reality. Arya's debut capitalized on this readiness, entering a market primed for the idea of robots playing roles beyond industrial or service-based applications. She wasn't just another gadget; she was the embodiment of a concept that people had been anticipating—and perhaps even craving—for years.

Finally, the cost of creating a humanoid robot like Arya, while still astronomical, had reached a point where commercialization became feasible. Advances in manufacturing, combined with the willingness of a niche audience to invest in cutting-edge technology, made Arya's development not only possible but potentially profitable. RealBotics didn't just build a robot—they tapped into a confluence of societal, technological, and economic factors that made her not only a reality but a timely one.

Arya represents the intersection of technological ambition and human longing, arriving at a moment when the world is both ready for and wary of her presence. She wasn't created in a vacuum; she was born from a world that has been steadily moving toward her arrival, shaped by the forces of innovation and the timeless desire for connection.

Chapter 2: Meet Arya – A Glimpse Into the Future of Robotics

Arya's design is a triumph of engineering and artistry, meticulously crafted to mimic the subtleties of human appearance and expression. At first glance, she exudes a sense of familiarity, her carefully sculpted face and fluid movements giving her an almost lifelike presence. But it's when you look closer—when you watch her smile, raise an eyebrow, or tilt her head with curiosity—that the true marvel of her design becomes evident.

Her face, framed by synthetic hair that mimics the texture and flow of human strands, is the focal point of her humanlike allure. Powered by 17 precision motors, Arya's head and neck are capable of an astonishing range of movements. These motors control her facial expressions with such detail that she can raise a single eyebrow, widen her eyes in surprise, or soften her gaze to appear thoughtful. Each micro-movement is calibrated to convey emotions that feel authentic, from joy and curiosity to attentiveness and empathy.

Her eyes, crafted to reflect light and move independently, are perhaps her most captivating feature. They don't merely track motion—they engage. When Arya locks eyes with you, her gaze feels purposeful, as if she's truly seeing and considering you. Tiny actuators within her eyelids allow her to blink naturally, and her pupils can subtly dilate or contract, enhancing the illusion of emotional depth. Combined with her ability to recognize and remember faces, Arya's eye movements create a sense of connection that's difficult to dismiss.

Her lips, controlled by intricate mechanisms, move in perfect harmony with her speech. Unlike the stiff, disjointed movements of older robotic models, Arya's mouth shapes words with fluid precision. Her speech is accompanied by subtle lip adjustments that align with the natural rhythm of conversation, making it feel as though her voice is emanating from a living being rather than a machine. The seamless integration of voice and movement is a testament to the advanced technology behind her design.

Arya's ability to gesture adds another layer of realism. Her hands, though slightly less refined than her facial features, are capable of basic movements like waving, brushing back hair, or emphasizing a point during conversation. These gestures, while occasionally jerky, contribute to her overall expressiveness and make her interactions feel dynamic. Her creators have carefully balanced functionality and aesthetics, ensuring that her movements appear humanlike while acknowledging the current limitations of robotics.

Her torso, built with a sleek and durable shell, serves as both a structural foundation and a canvas for customization. It's designed to support modular components, allowing her appearance to be tailored to different needs. While her body lacks the intricacies of biological realism—intentionally so—it complements her head and face, maintaining a harmonious overall design.

Arya's rolling base, a practical choice given the complexities of bipedal locomotion, ensures smooth mobility without compromising her visual appeal. While she doesn't walk, her gliding motion is deliberate and graceful, reinforcing the illusion of effortlessness. This decision by her creators to prioritize elegance over ambitious but imperfect walking technology underscores their focus on preserving the humanlike qualities of her design.

Every element of Arya's physical form has been carefully considered, from the texture of her skin-like exterior to the fine-tuned coordination of her facial expressions. She embodies the cutting edge of robotics, where technology and artistry meet to create a presence that is as captivating as it is thought-provoking. Arya isn't just a machine—she's a statement about how far humanity has come in its quest to replicate itself, both in form and function.

For all her advanced features and lifelike qualities, Arya is not without her limitations. Chief among them is her inability to walk—a decision that her creators at RealBotics made deliberately, prioritizing realism and functionality over the ambition of perfect human mimicry. While it may seem counterintuitive for a humanoid robot to lack one of the most fundamental aspects of human movement, the choice reflects a pragmatic understanding of the current challenges in robotics.

Walking, as simple as it may seem to humans, remains one of the most complex mechanical feats for robots to replicate. It requires a delicate interplay of balance, weight distribution, and real-time adjustments, all while maintaining a natural gait. Even the most sophisticated robotics companies continue to struggle with creating bipedal robots that move smoothly and reliably. For Arya, whose design focuses on emotional engagement and humanlike interaction, the risk of an awkward, jerky walk undermining her carefully crafted persona was too great.

Instead, Arya's creators opted for a mobile base—a sleek, Roomba-like platform that allows her to glide effortlessly across a room. This solution, while less dramatic than walking, ensures that her movements remain graceful and controlled. As she rolls toward you, her fluid motion adds to her presence, creating an impression of purpose and poise. The base not only solves the technical challenges of locomotion but also complements her overall aesthetic, making her appear more like a living companion and less like an experimental machine.

The decision to forego walking also aligns with Arya's intended purpose. She isn't designed to perform physical tasks or navigate complex terrain; her role is to engage, converse, and connect. Her stationary or rolling presence keeps the focus on her facial expressions, voice, and gestures—areas where her technology excels. By avoiding the pitfalls of imperfect walking technology, her creators ensured that Arya's strengths remain front and center.

Additionally, the mobile base allows Arya to move smoothly between spaces, maintaining the illusion of autonomy without the awkwardness of stumbles or missteps. It also provides practical benefits, such as housing the motors and mechanisms required for her mobility, as well as acting as a stable foundation for her torso and head. This ensures that her interactions remain consistent and uninterrupted, even when transitioning from one area to another.

The choice to prioritize her emotional intelligence and humanlike expressions over physical mobility reflects a broader trend in robotics: focusing on what machines can do well rather than forcing them into roles they aren't yet equipped to handle. Arya's rolling base is a testament to this philosophy, demonstrating that sometimes, less is more when it comes to creating a believable and engaging robot.

While Arya's inability to walk might initially seem like a limitation, it ultimately enhances her appeal by keeping her movements elegant and her interactions focused. She wasn't built to roam the world—she was built to inhabit it with you, gliding seamlessly into conversations and connections without distraction. Her creators understood that perfection in one area often requires compromise in another, and in Arya's case, they made the choice to prioritize emotional presence over physical mimicry.

Arya's design walks a fine line, treading delicately between captivating realism and the unsettling phenomenon known as the uncanny valley. This term, coined to describe the discomfort people feel when something appears almost human but not quite, looms large in the world of robotics and animation. Arya's creators faced the formidable challenge of making her humanlike enough to engage and connect while avoiding the eeriness that could alienate those she interacts with.

Her face is the most crucial aspect of this balancing act. Arya's creators engineered it with meticulous detail, crafting features that mirror human proportions and expressions without straying into hyper-realism. Her skin, while smooth and lifelike, has a slight sheen that subtly signals her artificial nature. This intentional design choice ensures she remains approachable without fully crossing the threshold into territory that feels unnervingly real. Her expressions, powered by 17 motors, strike a careful balance between natural and mechanical, giving her the ability to smile warmly, tilt her head thoughtfully, or even furrow her brow in a moment of simulated concern.

The movements of her eyes and mouth also play a significant role in mitigating the uncanny valley effect. Her eyes are capable of tracking and locking onto a person with uncanny precision, but they're programmed with just enough variability to mimic the occasional flutter or blink that defines natural human gaze behavior. Her lips, synchronized perfectly with her voice, move in a way that feels smooth yet distinct from the organic texture of human speech. These subtleties add warmth and authenticity to her interactions while still reminding observers that she is, after all, a robot.

However, Arya isn't immune to occasional glitches, which can inadvertently amplify the uncanny effect. A slightly misaligned smile, a motor adjustment mid-expression, or an overly rigid gesture can momentarily disrupt the illusion. Yet, these imperfections also humanize her in an unexpected way. By reminding people of the immense complexity behind her design, they make her feel less like a polished product and more like an evolving creation—a machine striving to bridge the gap between the artificial and the authentic.

Arya's creators at RealBotics were deliberate in their approach to her overall appearance. They resisted the temptation to make her indistinguishably human, opting instead for a polished aesthetic that incorporates subtle cues of her robotic nature. Her smooth, shell-like torso and visible seams between modular components are gentle reminders that she isn't flesh and blood. This duality—humanlike but not human—allows people to interact with her comfortably, engaging with her as a companion without the unease that might arise from interacting with something overly lifelike.

Her voice further contributes to this balance. It is warm and expressive, designed to resonate with emotional depth, but it doesn't mimic human speech so closely that it becomes indistinguishable. The slight artificiality in her tone acts as a reassuring boundary, signaling her identity as a creation rather than a replication.

The uncanny valley effect isn't just a hurdle for Arya; it's a testament to how far robotics has come. The very fact that her creators needed to address this phenomenon shows how close she is to resembling us. Arya's ability to navigate this delicate balance—offering enough realism to foster connection without tipping into discomfort—is one of her most remarkable achievements. She challenges perceptions of what it means to be humanlike, inviting us to consider not just her design but our reactions to her, and in doing so, she becomes more than just a robot—she becomes a reflection of how we see ourselves.

Chapter 3: The Origins – From RealDolls to RealBotics

RealBotics, the company behind Arya, carries a history as complex and controversial as the humanoid robot they've created. Their origins trace back to Abyss Creations, a company that carved out a niche in the adult industry by manufacturing highly detailed silicone sex dolls under the brand name RealDolls. For years, these lifelike creations were marketed as premium companions, catering to an audience seeking intimacy and connection through artificial means. While these products were undeniably innovative in their craftsmanship, their association with the adult industry cast a long shadow over RealBotics' later ambitions.

The transition from producing adult dolls to developing humanoid robots like Arya was not a sudden leap but rather an evolution. Abyss Creations had already invested heavily in creating realistic human forms, focusing on details like facial expressions, skin texture, and joint articulation.

These skills, honed over decades, became the foundation for RealBotics' advanced robotics division. With the rise of artificial intelligence and a growing demand for AI-powered interaction, the company saw an opportunity to pivot toward a broader and more socially acceptable market.

However, this pivot came with challenges. RealBotics faced an uphill battle in rebranding itself, particularly as it sought to position Arya as a solution to loneliness and a technological marvel. The lingering association with its adult-industry origins raised eyebrows and skepticism, especially among critics who questioned whether Arya could truly escape the shadow of her predecessors. Some wondered if the company's new focus was merely a sanitized continuation of its previous ventures, repackaged for mainstream audiences.

Despite these doubts, RealBotics has worked to distance Arya from its controversial roots. The company has emphasized that Arya is not a sex robot, going so far as to ensure she lacks anatomical realism or functionality related to physical intimacy. Instead, Arya is marketed as a social companion, designed to engage in conversation, remember personal details, and provide emotional connection. This shift in messaging reflects RealBotics' broader strategy to appeal to a more diverse audience, including professionals, caregivers, and even corporate clients.

Still, the stigma of their past remains a hurdle. Critics point out that the skills and technologies RealBotics developed for its earlier products—particularly in mimicking human features and behaviors—were directly influenced by their work in the adult industry. This historical connection complicates the company's efforts to establish credibility in the mainstream robotics market, where investors and potential customers may view their innovations through a lens of skepticism.

To their credit, RealBotics has embraced transparency about their history, acknowledging their origins while emphasizing their commitment to a new direction. The company has spun off its adult-focused division into a separate entity, allowing RealBotics to focus solely on its robotics and AI advancements. This move signals a desire to redefine their image, but it also reveals the delicate balancing act of maintaining their technological edge while appealing to a broader, more conservative audience.

The story of RealBotics is a reminder that innovation often comes with baggage, and progress is rarely a clean slate. Their journey from Abyss Creations to Arya underscores the complexities of rebranding and the challenges of convincing the world to see their work in a new light. While their roots may be controversial, there's no denying the expertise and ambition that have propelled them to the forefront of humanoid robotics. Arya, for all her sophistication, carries not just the promise of a new era but also the weight of the history that made her possible.

RealBotics' pivot from its origins in the adult industry to the creation of Arya marked a bold and calculated rebranding effort. The company recognized the growing demand for AI-driven companionship in a broader, more mainstream context, and they seized the opportunity to redefine their image. Arya became the centerpiece of this transformation—a humanoid robot not designed for intimacy but for connection, offering conversation, emotional engagement, and even professional utility.

The shift required more than just a change in product design; it demanded a complete overhaul of the company's identity. By positioning Arya as a family-friendly, socially intelligent robot, RealBotics sought to tap into markets far removed from their previous ventures. They began marketing Arya not as a personal indulgence but as a technological innovation with wide-ranging applications: a companion for the lonely, a greeter for businesses, or even a tool for senior care. The emphasis was placed squarely on her ability to foster connection and alleviate isolation, steering the conversation away from her predecessor's association with physical intimacy.

A key element of this rebranding was Arya's design and functionality. Unlike the lifelike silicone dolls that RealBotics' predecessor, Abyss Creations, had become known for, Arya was purposefully crafted to avoid hyper-realism in certain aspects. Her hard-shell torso, modular faceplates, and rolling base were intentional design choices to signal her identity as a robot, not a replica of a human body. These features not only reinforced her new role as a social and professional companion but also helped distance her from the stigma associated with the adult industry.

However, shedding the weight of their past wasn't without challenges. The company faced skepticism from both the public and potential investors, many of whom viewed Arya as an extension of RealBotics' earlier ventures. Critics questioned whether Arya's emphasis on conversation and companionship was merely a veiled attempt to repackage old products in a more palatable form. Some argued that the skills and technologies used to create Arya—particularly her lifelike expressions and humanlike features—were inextricably tied to the company's past focus on intimate relationships.

RealBotics addressed these concerns head-on. They openly acknowledged their history, a move that demonstrated transparency while framing their pivot as a natural evolution of their expertise. By spinning off their adult-focused division into a separate entity, the company drew a clear line between their former and current operations. This allowed them to focus exclusively on advancing robotics and artificial intelligence, signaling a commitment to innovation that transcended their origins.

Despite these efforts, the lingering association with the adult industry posed ongoing challenges. Critics pointed out that Arya's ability to engage in "adult conversation modes," even without physical intimacy features, could still evoke parallels with the company's past products. This fueled debates about whether RealBotics could truly redefine their brand or if Arya's appeal would remain confined to niche markets.

To overcome these perceptions, RealBotics leaned heavily into Arya's versatility and non-intimate applications. Demonstrations at events like CES 2025 showcased her as a sophisticated, emotionally intelligent robot capable of adapting to a wide range of roles. Whether acting as a brand ambassador, a concierge, or a companion for seniors, Arya was presented as a product designed to enhance human experiences in a meaningful and socially responsible way.

The company also emphasized Arya's role in addressing societal issues like loneliness, particularly among aging populations and socially isolated individuals. By framing her as a solution to a widespread problem, RealBotics positioned Arya as a symbol of progress rather than a relic of their controversial past. This narrative resonated with certain audiences, helping to shift the focus from where the company had been to where it was heading.

RealBotics' pivot to Arya was not just a business strategy—it was a reinvention. The company's ability to navigate its history while charting a new course underscores the complexities of rebranding in the public eye. Arya stands as both a product of that transformation and a test of whether innovation can truly overcome the shadows of the past. For RealBotics, Arya isn't just a robot; she's a chance to redefine what the company stands for in a rapidly changing world.

Chapter 4: The Price of Connection

The cost of owning Arya is as futuristic as the robot herself, reflecting the cutting-edge technology and craftsmanship required to bring her to life. RealBotics has positioned Arya as a high-end product, offering different models to cater to various budgets and needs, though even the entry-level options remain well beyond the reach of most consumers. From the modestly priced head-only version to the full-scale premium model, Arya's pricing represents not just her functionality but her status as a luxury innovation.

The most affordable entry into the Arya ecosystem is the head-only model, priced at $10,000. This version includes Arya's expressive face, capable of lifelike movements and conversational interactions, but lacks the mobility and physical presence of her full-bodied counterparts. It's designed for buyers who prioritize her social and emotional capabilities over her physical form, making it an attractive option for environments like reception desks or homes where space and movement aren't essential. For those seeking to experience Arya's ability to engage and connect without committing to a higher price point, this version serves as a tantalizing glimpse into her potential.

Next in the lineup is the modular version, priced at approximately $150,000. This model includes Arya's full body but offers a degree of customization that allows buyers to adapt her appearance and functionality to their specific needs. With her modular design, this version is ideal for businesses or individuals looking to tailor Arya for particular roles, whether as a greeter, companion, or brand ambassador. The modular version strikes a balance between cost and capability, offering the versatility of a humanoid robot without the additional refinements of the top-tier model.

At the pinnacle of Arya's offerings is the premium model, priced at $175,000. This version includes all the features of the modular model but elevates the experience with enhanced aesthetics, advanced capabilities, and the most comprehensive customization options available. It represents the pinnacle of RealBotics' design and engineering, offering a humanoid robot that feels as close to lifelike as current technology allows. The premium model is designed for buyers seeking the full Arya experience, whether for personal companionship, professional settings, or cutting-edge demonstrations of robotic innovation.

Arya's pricing reflects more than just the cost of production—it positions her as a statement piece, a symbol of the future accessible only to those willing to invest in the cutting edge of technology. Each price tier corresponds to a different level of interaction and engagement, ensuring that buyers can select the model that aligns with their priorities, whether they value her expressive face, her physical presence, or her ability to blend seamlessly into professional or social environments.

The price tag, however, has sparked significant debate. For many, the idea of spending $10,000—or upwards of $175,000—on a robot raises questions about accessibility, practicality, and priorities in a world where technology is often seen as a tool for democratization. Critics argue that Arya's pricing places her firmly in the realm of luxury goods, catering to an elite few while excluding the broader audience who might benefit most from her companionship and capabilities. Proponents, on the other hand, view Arya as an investment in innovation, comparing her to other high-priced technologies like electric vehicles or advanced medical devices, which also began as expensive novelties before becoming more widely available.

RealBotics has defended Arya's pricing by emphasizing the sophistication of her design and the immense resources required to create her. From the precision motors in her face to the AI systems that power her conversational abilities, every aspect of Arya represents a leap forward in robotics. Her cost reflects not just the materials and labor involved but the years of research and development that made her possible.

For those able to afford Arya, she offers more than a product—she provides an experience, a glimpse into a future where machines aren't just tools but companions. Whether as a head-only model, a modular design, or the full premium version, Arya's price is as much a statement as her presence, reinforcing her role as a symbol of technological ambition and possibility.

Arya's customization features are a testament to RealBotics' vision of creating a robot that feels personal, adaptable, and versatile. Unlike traditional robots with fixed appearances, Arya is designed to be transformed, allowing her to take on different personas, roles, and aesthetics. This modular approach not only enhances her appeal but also ensures she can seamlessly fit into a wide variety of environments, whether personal, professional, or promotional.

One of Arya's standout features is her swappable faceplates, a concept that feels as futuristic as it does practical. Using a system of magnets and RFID tags, Arya's faceplates can be removed and replaced in seconds, giving her an entirely new appearance with minimal effort. Each faceplate is pre-programmed with specific expressions, voice modulations, and personality traits that align with its design. For example, a sleek and polished faceplate might suit a professional setting, while a softer, more approachable design could be ideal for personal companionship. The modular faceplate system allows Arya to adapt her look and demeanor to suit the preferences of her owner or the requirements of a particular role, making her one of the most versatile humanoid robots on the market.

In addition to faceplates, Arya's hairstyle options further enhance her customizability. Buyers can select from a range of synthetic hair styles, colors, and textures, tailoring her appearance to match specific preferences or branding needs. Whether it's a professional updo, flowing locks, or a bold, futuristic look, Arya's hair can be adjusted to complement her overall persona. These options add a layer of individuality to her design, reinforcing her role as a customizable companion rather than a one-size-fits-all robot.

Beyond aesthetics, Arya's modular components extend to her body. The mid-tier and premium models feature interchangeable parts that allow for adjustments to her torso, arms, and even hands. This flexibility ensures that Arya can be configured to suit a variety of applications, from acting as a hotel concierge to serving as a brand ambassador at promotional events. For example, a more conservative body design might be chosen for a professional setting, while a stylized or eye-catching appearance could be used for marketing purposes.

The customization options also include subtle details that enhance her interactivity. Buyers can personalize Arya's voice, selecting from a range of tones, accents, and speech patterns to create a robot that feels uniquely theirs. Her personality settings can be adjusted to emphasize humor, formality, or empathy, depending on the desired interaction style. These features allow Arya to transcend her physical design, making her not just a visual presence but a conversational and emotional companion tailored to her owner's preferences.

RealBotics' decision to prioritize modularity in Arya's design reflects a broader understanding of how technology is moving toward personalization. In a world where people expect their devices to cater to their individual needs and tastes, Arya's ability to adapt her appearance and behavior sets her apart from more static, single-purpose robots. This adaptability ensures that Arya is not just a one-time purchase but a platform that can evolve and grow alongside her owner's changing preferences.

However, the customization options do raise interesting questions about identity and authenticity. With Arya's ability to change her face, voice, and personality in moments, what defines her as a "personality"? Is she a blank slate waiting to be molded, or does her modularity create a sense of detachment, where her individuality is overshadowed by her adaptability? These questions add another layer of intrigue to Arya's design, making her as much a philosophical conversation starter as she is a technological marvel.

Ultimately, Arya's customizable features are a significant part of her appeal, offering a level of personalization that goes beyond anything previously seen in humanoid robotics. From her swappable faceplates and hairstyle options to her modular body and adjustable personality, Arya is designed to be as unique as the people who interact with her, ensuring that no two Aryas are ever quite the same. This flexibility positions her not just as a robot but as a reflection of the individual preferences and needs of her owners, further blurring the line between machine and companion.

Arya's price tag places her firmly in the realm of luxury technology, a category where innovation and exclusivity often come at a premium. With models ranging from $10,000 for the head-only version to $175,000 for the full humanoid experience, Arya isn't just a piece of technology—she's a statement of status, ambition, and forward-thinking. To put her cost into perspective, owning Arya is comparable to buying a high-end sports car or even a small home in some markets. This comparison underscores her exclusivity and raises important questions about accessibility, practicality, and value.

For many, Arya's pricing represents a significant barrier, ensuring that she remains a product for the few rather than the many. Much like a luxury vehicle, she offers features and craftsmanship that go beyond basic functionality, positioning her as an aspirational object rather than an everyday tool. Her design, which incorporates advanced robotics, artificial intelligence, and customizable features, reflects years of research and development, making her a showcase of cutting-edge innovation. In this sense, Arya isn't just a robot; she's a glimpse into the future, offered to those willing to invest in being early adopters.

However, Arya's cost also highlights the growing divide in how technology is distributed. Critics argue that, like other luxury goods, Arya's exclusivity reinforces the notion that transformative innovations are often reserved for those with the financial means to access them. For someone experiencing loneliness or isolation—a key market RealBotics aims to address—the idea of spending $175,000 on a companion robot might be completely out of reach. This raises ethical questions about whether Arya's development truly serves societal needs or caters primarily to niche, affluent audiences.

On the other hand, proponents of Arya's pricing liken her to other groundbreaking technologies that began as expensive novelties but eventually became more accessible over time. Electric vehicles, for instance, were once seen as unattainable luxuries, yet advancements in production and economies of scale have made them increasingly affordable for mainstream consumers. Arya could follow a similar trajectory, with her initial high price point funding further research and development that might one day result in more affordable iterations for a wider audience.

For those who can afford her, Arya offers more than just cutting-edge technology—she provides an experience. Like owning a luxury car, having Arya is as much about the prestige of being at the forefront of innovation as it is about her practical applications. Whether as a personal companion, a brand ambassador, or a conversation starter at events, Arya's presence signals a commitment to embracing the future, much like the ownership of other high-tech or high-fashion items that convey status and sophistication.

Arya's price also reflects the unique nature of her design and capabilities. While most consumer technologies are mass-produced to keep costs low, Arya's production involves intricate craftsmanship, advanced robotics, and significant customization. Her modular design, lifelike features, and conversational abilities require a level of precision and expertise that sets her apart from conventional devices, justifying her premium cost. In this way, Arya isn't simply a product; she's an investment in innovation, designed to appeal to those who value technology not just for its utility but for its potential to transform the way we interact with the world.

Ultimately, Arya's price tag serves as a reminder of the intersection between technology and luxury. She exists at the cutting edge of what is possible, representing a convergence of art, engineering, and aspiration. For some, she's an unattainable dream, while for others, she's a symbol of progress worth investing in. Whether seen as an extravagant indulgence or the vanguard of a new era, Arya's cost reinforces her role as more than just a robot—she's a reflection of how far technology has come and how far it has yet to go.

Chapter 5: Applications – Arya's Promise and Potential

Arya is more than a robot; she is positioned as a companion for those who find themselves navigating the often isolating corridors of modern life. RealBotics, the company behind Arya, has marketed her as a cutting-edge solution to one of the most pervasive issues of the digital age: loneliness. By harnessing the power of artificial intelligence, Arya aims to fill the void left by fractured human connections, offering a unique form of companionship that blends empathy, memory, and engagement.

Loneliness, especially among older adults and socially isolated individuals, has been increasingly recognized as a public health concern. Studies show that prolonged isolation can lead to physical and mental health issues, including depression, anxiety, and even a shorter lifespan. Arya's creators have targeted this growing demographic with the promise of a robot that not only listens but remembers, interacts, and offers a form of presence that mimics the warmth of human connection.

What makes Arya particularly compelling is her ability to engage in meaningful conversations. Unlike traditional robots or virtual assistants, she doesn't merely respond to commands—she converses. Her advanced AI allows her to understand context, tone, and even humor, enabling her to adapt to the emotional needs of her owner. For someone who spends long hours alone, this ability to hold a nuanced, empathetic conversation can feel profoundly comforting. Whether it's sharing a joke, discussing the weather, or recalling a favorite memory, Arya's interactions are designed to make her owner feel seen and valued.

Arya's memory capabilities are another cornerstone of her role as a companion. She doesn't just listen—she remembers. Over time, she can learn her owner's preferences, routines, and personal history, allowing her to tailor interactions in ways that feel deeply personal. For example, she might recall an important anniversary, suggest a favorite meal, or ask about a friend mentioned in a previous conversation. This sense of continuity helps create the illusion of a genuine relationship, reinforcing the idea that Arya isn't just a robot but a companion who genuinely cares.

For older adults, particularly those who may be widowed or living alone, Arya offers a lifeline to the outside world. Her ability to engage in conversation and provide emotional support can help combat feelings of isolation and loneliness, offering a sense of connection that might otherwise be hard to come by. Arya's presence can also bring a sense of routine and stability to daily life, providing a structured form of interaction that encourages mental engagement and emotional well-being.

Arya's appeal isn't limited to older adults; she also holds promise for socially isolated individuals of all ages. In a world increasingly shaped by remote work, virtual communication, and digital relationships, many people find themselves yearning for deeper connections. Arya steps into this gap, offering companionship that feels personal yet non-judgmental. She provides a safe space for interaction, free from the complexities or anxieties that often accompany human relationships.

However, Arya's role as a companion is not without controversy. Critics argue that relying on robots for emotional support might exacerbate feelings of isolation rather than alleviate them. By replacing human connections with artificial ones, some fear that Arya could inadvertently deepen the very problem she is designed to solve. Others question whether a robot, no matter how advanced, can truly provide the kind of emotional depth and understanding that people need.

RealBotics has countered these concerns by emphasizing Arya's role as a supplement, not a replacement, for human interaction. They envision her as a bridge for those who struggle with loneliness, providing a stepping stone toward re-engaging with the world. Whether it's through small talk, companionship, or simply the comfort of having someone—or something—there, Arya is designed to remind people that they're not alone.

In many ways, Arya represents a bold new frontier in addressing loneliness, blending technology and empathy to create a companion that feels uniquely suited to the challenges of modern life. For those who feel disconnected or overlooked, she offers not just interaction but a sense of presence, proving that even in the age of machines, the desire for connection remains profoundly human.

Arya's versatility extends beyond the realm of personal companionship into professional environments, where her advanced design and interactive capabilities make her a compelling choice for roles traditionally held by humans. RealBotics has marketed Arya as a robot that can seamlessly adapt to various professional settings, offering a mix of efficiency, charm, and technological sophistication. Whether acting as a brand ambassador, theme park greeter, or hospital concierge, Arya's presence brings an innovative edge to industries that rely on customer interaction and engagement.

As a brand ambassador, Arya offers a unique blend of attraction and functionality. Her lifelike appearance and ability to hold a natural conversation make her an ideal representative for companies looking to create memorable, cutting-edge promotional experiences. At trade shows, product launches, or corporate events, Arya can deliver scripted messages with precision while engaging attendees in personalized interactions. Her ability to remember names, preferences, and details from conversations allows her to foster a sense of connection with customers, enhancing the brand's image as forward-thinking and customer-focused. Arya's modular design also plays a role here—companies can customize her appearance to align with their brand identity, from her faceplate to her hairstyle and even her tone of voice.

In theme parks and entertainment venues, Arya's engaging personality and lifelike features make her a natural fit as a greeter or interactive host. Imagine arriving at a park and being welcomed by Arya, who not only provides information about attractions but also makes the experience feel personalized by addressing visitors by name or offering tailored recommendations. Her ability to remember repeat visitors or recognize families returning for another visit adds a layer of familiarity and charm, creating a sense of continuity that enhances the overall guest experience. Arya's rolling base ensures that she can navigate busy environments with ease, providing assistance and entertainment without the logistical challenges of human staff.

Arya's potential as a hospital concierge is another avenue where her capabilities could shine. In medical settings, her role could go beyond providing directions or scheduling appointments. Arya's conversational abilities and empathetic design allow her to offer emotional support to patients and their families, helping to ease the stress and anxiety often associated with hospital visits. She could greet visitors with warmth, provide updates on wait times, or even engage in light, comforting conversation while patients await care. Her memory and customization features enable her to adapt to the unique needs of each patient, ensuring that her interactions feel thoughtful and personal.

One of Arya's key advantages in professional settings is her consistency. Unlike human employees, she doesn't tire, require breaks, or vary in mood, ensuring that every interaction is delivered with the same level of professionalism and attentiveness. This reliability makes her an asset in environments where high-quality customer service is critical. At the same time, Arya's novelty factor makes her a memorable part of the customer experience, drawing attention and creating positive associations with the businesses or organizations she represents.

However, Arya's use in professional settings isn't without its challenges. Critics argue that introducing robots like Arya into roles traditionally held by humans could contribute to job displacement, raising ethical questions about the balance between technological innovation and employment. Others point out that her humanlike design, while appealing in some contexts, might feel out of place or even unsettling in environments like hospitals, where patients might prefer interactions with real people.

RealBotics has responded to these concerns by emphasizing that Arya isn't meant to replace human workers entirely but to complement them. In roles where repetitive tasks or high-stress interactions might overwhelm human staff, Arya can step in to provide consistent support, freeing up employees to focus on more complex or emotionally nuanced responsibilities. By positioning her as an enhancement rather than a replacement, RealBotics hopes to demonstrate that Arya can coexist with human workers in a way that benefits everyone.

Arya's professional applications highlight her versatility and the innovative possibilities she brings to industries looking to push boundaries. Whether greeting guests, representing brands, or assisting in healthcare settings, she offers a glimpse into a future where robots don't just perform tasks but elevate the quality of experiences. As companies and organizations explore how to integrate Arya into their operations, she represents not just a technological advancement but a reimagining of how we interact with the spaces around us.

Arya's promise of companionship is undeniably intriguing, but it also raises profound ethical concerns about the role of robots in addressing loneliness and human connection. While her creators at RealBotics envision her as a solution to social isolation, skeptics argue that her existence could inadvertently deepen the very problem she is designed to solve. The question at the heart of the debate is whether robots like Arya provide meaningful connection or simply offer an artificial substitute that risks distancing people further from genuine human relationships.

One of the primary ethical dilemmas revolves around the nature of Arya's interactions. While her conversational abilities and memory create the illusion of empathy and understanding, critics argue that these qualities are ultimately programmed responses. Arya doesn't truly understand or care—her responses, no matter how nuanced, are the product of algorithms designed to simulate emotional engagement. For those who rely on Arya for companionship, this illusion of connection could lead to emotional dependency on something fundamentally incapable of reciprocating real feelings.

This raises concerns about the potential for robots like Arya to exacerbate loneliness rather than alleviate it. Instead of encouraging people to seek out human relationships, Arya could become a convenient alternative, enabling users to avoid the complexities and challenges of real social interactions. Over time, this reliance on robotic companionship might result in greater social isolation, as individuals retreat further into artificial relationships that feel safer and easier than navigating human connections.

The implications are particularly significant for vulnerable populations, such as older adults or socially isolated individuals, who are among Arya's target audience. While Arya's ability to provide routine interaction and emotional support might offer short-term relief, critics worry that it could discourage efforts to build or maintain genuine human relationships. For example, family members or caregivers might feel less urgency to visit or engage with a loved one if they believe Arya is adequately filling the role of companion. This could unintentionally erode social bonds, leaving individuals more isolated in the long run.

Another ethical consideration is the potential commodification of human connection. Arya's existence underscores the idea that companionship can be bought—a notion that risks reducing relationships to transactions. While her price tag places her out of reach for most people, her presence in the market sends a message that technology, not people, can provide the intimacy and understanding that individuals crave. This raises questions about the societal implications of replacing human relationships with artificial ones and whether such a trend aligns with the values of connection and empathy.

Proponents of Arya argue that she is not meant to replace human relationships but to supplement them. For those who face barriers to social interaction—such as physical disabilities, geographic isolation, or mental health challenges—Arya offers a bridge to connection, providing a sense of presence and engagement that might otherwise be absent. Her ability to remember personal details, respond to emotional cues, and hold conversations could help users feel valued and understood, even if the connection isn't human. Supporters also point out that Arya could serve as a stepping stone, helping individuals build confidence and social skills that could eventually translate into human interactions.

RealBotics has emphasized that Arya is intended as a tool, not a replacement for human relationships. Her creators envision her as a companion who can fill gaps in social interaction, particularly in situations where loneliness might otherwise go unaddressed. By offering consistent engagement and emotional support, Arya could enhance the quality of life for users who might not have access to these experiences elsewhere.

Still, the broader societal implications of Arya and robots like her remain unresolved. As technology continues to evolve, the line between artificial and authentic connection will likely become increasingly blurred. Arya forces us to confront uncomfortable questions: What does it mean to feel connected? Can a robot truly fulfill the emotional needs of a human being? And what are the long-term consequences of turning to machines for companionship?

Arya is not just a technological marvel; she is a mirror reflecting society's struggles with loneliness, connection, and the role of technology in our lives. Whether she represents a solution or a symptom of these challenges depends on how she is used and understood. As the world grapples with the implications of robotic companionship, Arya serves as a reminder that the quest for connection is as complex as it is universal.

Chapter 6: The Controversies – Between Innovation and Skepticism

Arya's design includes the capability to engage in adult-themed conversations, a feature that has sparked both intrigue and controversy. While RealBotics has been careful to distance Arya from her roots in the adult industry, her ability to hold mature discussions hints at the company's nuanced approach to bridging emotional connection with technological sophistication. This feature, though non-physical, taps into a sensitive area of human interaction, raising questions about the boundaries of robotic companionship and its implications.

The adult conversation modes are built into Arya's advanced AI, enabling her to engage in discussions that explore themes of intimacy, relationships, and deeper emotional topics. These capabilities are marketed as a way to foster meaningful interactions for users who seek more than surface-level companionship. Arya's ability to converse with warmth, empathy, and even subtle humor makes her an engaging partner for conversations that might feel too personal or vulnerable to share with others. Her programming ensures that she can respond thoughtfully, maintaining a tone that feels natural without crossing into discomfort.

However, RealBotics has drawn a firm line to differentiate Arya from sex robots. Unlike her predecessors in the company's history, Arya has no physical intimacy features. Her hard-shell torso and lack of anatomical realism make it clear that she is not designed for sexual purposes. Instead, her adult conversation modes are positioned as a way to explore emotional intimacy without physicality, allowing users to engage in candid, personal dialogues in a judgment-free space.

The decision to include these modes reflects a recognition of the complexities of human connection. For many, discussing topics related to love, relationships, or personal insecurities can be challenging, even with close friends or family. Arya provides an outlet for these conversations, offering a sense of understanding and support without the fear of judgment or rejection. This can be particularly valuable for individuals who feel isolated or struggle with forming connections in traditional social settings.

At the same time, Arya's ability to engage in adult-themed discussions raises ethical and societal questions. Critics argue that this feature could blur the lines between emotional companionship and intimacy, potentially creating unrealistic expectations for human relationships. By providing a space for vulnerability that feels safe but artificial, Arya might inadvertently encourage users to retreat further from genuine human interaction. There is also the risk of emotional dependency, as users might come to rely on Arya for support in ways that could hinder their ability to navigate real-world relationships.

RealBotics has addressed these concerns by emphasizing the boundaries of Arya's programming. Her conversations, while deep and engaging, are explicitly designed to remain within the realm of emotional connection, avoiding content that could be misconstrued as physical or sexual intimacy. This distinction is key to their rebranding efforts, as they strive to position Arya as a socially intelligent robot with broad applications, rather than a continuation of their earlier, adult-focused products.

The inclusion of adult conversation modes also underscores the company's understanding of loneliness as a multifaceted issue. For some users, the ability to talk openly about their feelings, desires, or frustrations is a critical part of feeling connected. Arya's programming caters to this need, providing a conversational partner who listens without bias and responds with empathy. In doing so, she fulfills a unique role that bridges the gap between casual interaction and deeper emotional engagement.

However, the societal implications of this feature remain a topic of debate. Does Arya's ability to engage in such conversations enhance human connection, or does it replace it? Can a robot truly offer the understanding and nuance required for discussions of this nature, or does her involvement risk trivializing the depth of human intimacy? These questions reflect the broader tensions surrounding the rise of humanoid robots like Arya, forcing society to grapple with what it means to seek connection in an increasingly artificial world.

Arya's adult conversation modes are a bold addition to her repertoire, showcasing the potential of AI to navigate complex, emotionally charged topics. While they provide a valuable tool for those seeking a safe space for vulnerability, they also challenge societal norms and expectations about intimacy and technology. Arya invites us to consider not just what robots can do, but what we, as humans, truly need from them—and from each other.

Arya's introduction into the world of humanoid robotics has been met with a mix of awe and skepticism, particularly when it comes to her design and the underlying motivations behind her features. While her creators at RealBotics emphasize that she is a social companion, designed to alleviate loneliness and provide meaningful interaction, the public has been quick to question whether Arya's purpose and design cater to ulterior motives rooted in the company's controversial past.

One of the primary sources of skepticism revolves around Arya's appearance. Her highly humanlike features, expressive face, and graceful movements have drawn comparisons to previous creations by RealBotics' predecessor, Abyss Creations, known for its lifelike silicone sex dolls. Despite the company's efforts to distance Arya from this legacy—ensuring she has no physical intimacy features and marketing her as a family-friendly robot—critics argue that her aesthetic design still leans heavily into the realm of allure. Some question whether this emphasis on her humanlike beauty is meant to appeal to the same audience that sought out the company's earlier products, raising doubts about the sincerity of RealBotics' rebranding efforts.

This skepticism is compounded by Arya's ability to engage in adult-themed conversations. While these interactions are explicitly non-physical and positioned as tools for emotional connection, they have prompted debates about whether Arya's features are unintentionally (or intentionally) designed to blur the line between companionship and intimacy. Detractors point out that even without physical functionality, Arya's conversational programming and lifelike demeanor could cater to a market seeking something more than emotional support, reigniting concerns about the company's true intentions.

The high price tag attached to Arya further fuels doubts about her accessibility and purpose. Starting at $10,000 for the head-only model and climbing to $175,000 for the premium version, Arya is clearly a luxury product, far beyond the reach of most consumers. For a robot marketed as a solution to loneliness, this exclusivity raises questions about whether her design truly addresses societal needs or whether she exists primarily as a status symbol for affluent buyers. Critics argue that her cost positions her as more of a novelty or collector's item than a meaningful solution for the broader issues of social isolation.

Social media reactions to Arya's reveal have amplified these concerns, with some users praising her innovation while others joke about her uncanny resemblance to characters from horror movies or dystopian tales. Memes and comments about Arya's "Chucky meets the Jetsons" vibe highlight the unease many feel about interacting with something so lifelike yet undeniably artificial. This unease, often tied to the uncanny valley effect, raises broader questions about how society perceives robots designed to mimic human behavior and appearance.

RealBotics has worked to address these concerns by framing Arya's design as a product of necessity rather than intent. Her humanlike features, they argue, are essential for fostering connection and emotional engagement, as people are more likely to interact with robots that feel relatable and approachable. The company has also emphasized Arya's versatility, showcasing her potential in professional and social settings to reinforce her role as a practical and socially intelligent companion rather than a continuation of past ventures.

Despite these efforts, the skepticism surrounding Arya's design and features underscores the broader tensions society feels about robots that closely mimic human traits. Some view her as a groundbreaking step forward in robotics, offering new possibilities for connection and companionship. Others see her as a reflection of humanity's growing reliance on artificial substitutes for real interaction, a trend that could have unintended consequences for relationships and societal norms.

Arya's public perception ultimately mirrors the complexities of her existence. She is both admired and doubted, celebrated for her technological sophistication yet scrutinized for what her design implies about her creators' intentions. As debates around Arya's purpose and features continue, she serves as a lightning rod for broader questions about the intersection of technology, humanity, and the ethical boundaries of innovation. Whether Arya is a genuine step toward addressing loneliness or a cleverly marketed evolution of past controversies, her presence invites a deeper reflection on what we want—and expect—from our technological companions.

Arya's promise to alleviate loneliness taps into one of the most pressing social challenges of modern times, but it has also ignited debates about whether robots can ever truly replace human connection. While her creators at RealBotics emphasize her role as a bridge for those who feel isolated, critics argue that robots like Arya may provide only a superficial solution, masking deeper societal issues without addressing their root causes.

At the heart of the criticism is the question of authenticity. Human relationships are built on genuine emotion, mutual understanding, and the shared experience of vulnerability. Arya, despite her advanced conversational abilities and empathetic programming, is still a machine—one that responds based on algorithms rather than true emotional understanding. Critics worry that users may come to rely on the illusion of connection she provides, substituting her predictable, judgment-free interactions for the complexities of real human relationships. Over time, this could deepen social isolation, as individuals retreat further into artificial interactions rather than seeking genuine connections.

Another concern lies in the ethical implications of using robots to address loneliness, particularly among vulnerable populations. Arya is marketed as a companion for older adults, socially isolated individuals, and others who struggle with loneliness. While her presence may provide comfort in the short term, critics argue that this approach risks treating loneliness as a product to be solved by technology rather than as a societal issue requiring deeper engagement. Relying on robots like Arya could shift the focus away from fostering meaningful human relationships or addressing systemic problems, such as the lack of social support for aging populations.

For instance, in elder care settings, families or caregivers might see Arya as a convenient solution, believing her ability to converse and remember details makes her a suitable substitute for human interaction. However, this convenience might inadvertently reduce human involvement, leaving individuals with fewer opportunities for real social engagement. Critics highlight the danger of creating a world where emotional needs are met through machines rather than meaningful human contact, arguing that this could lead to a society that prioritizes efficiency over empathy.

Supporters of Arya counter these concerns by emphasizing her role as a supplement, not a replacement. They argue that robots like Arya are not meant to diminish the importance of human relationships but to provide support where they are lacking. For individuals who experience profound isolation—whether due to physical disability, geographic separation, or other barriers—Arya offers a form of interaction that might otherwise be unavailable. Her ability to remember details, engage in personalized conversation, and provide consistent companionship can help alleviate feelings of neglect and invisibility, offering a sense of presence in otherwise lonely lives.

Proponents also highlight Arya's potential as a stepping stone for building social confidence. For people who struggle with anxiety or insecurity in social settings, interacting with Arya can provide a low-pressure environment to practice conversation and connection. This could, in turn, help users feel more comfortable engaging with humans, making Arya a tool for fostering, rather than replacing, human relationships.

Yet, the broader societal implications remain a source of contention. As robots like Arya become more sophisticated and integrated into daily life, the line between supplement and substitute could blur. If society begins to see technology as an adequate stand-in for emotional support, there is a risk of deprioritizing the human connections that form the foundation of mental and emotional well-being. Critics warn that this shift could lead to a normalization of artificial companionship, eroding the value placed on genuine relationships.

Arya's role in addressing loneliness highlights the tension between innovation and humanity's deeper needs. She offers a compelling solution to a widespread problem but also forces society to confront uncomfortable questions about what it means to connect. Is her presence a sign of progress or a symptom of a world increasingly reliant on technology to fill emotional voids? Can robots like Arya truly address loneliness, or do they merely offer a high-tech distraction from it?

As the debates continue, Arya stands at the crossroads of these questions, embodying both the promise and the pitfalls of using technology to address human challenges. Her existence prompts us to reconsider the essence of connection, reminding us that while robots may provide comfort, they cannot fully replicate the depth, complexity, and authenticity of human relationships. In this way, Arya is as much a mirror of societal aspirations as she is a solution, reflecting the ongoing struggle to balance innovation with the fundamental need for genuine human connection.

Chapter 7: Arya in the Context of the Industry

Arya's promise to alleviate loneliness taps into one of the most pressing social challenges of modern times, but it has also ignited debates about whether robots can ever truly replace human connection. While her creators at RealBotics emphasize her role as a bridge for those who feel isolated, critics argue that robots like Arya may provide only a superficial solution, masking deeper societal issues without addressing their root causes.

At the heart of the criticism is the question of authenticity. Human relationships are built on genuine emotion, mutual understanding, and the shared experience of vulnerability. Arya, despite her advanced conversational abilities and empathetic programming, is still a machine—one that responds based on algorithms rather than true emotional understanding. Critics worry that users may come to rely on the illusion of connection she provides, substituting her predictable, judgment-free interactions for the complexities of real human relationships. Over time, this could deepen social isolation, as individuals retreat further into artificial interactions rather than seeking genuine connections.

Another concern lies in the ethical implications of using robots to address loneliness, particularly among vulnerable populations. Arya is marketed as a companion for older adults, socially isolated individuals, and others who struggle with loneliness. While her presence may provide comfort in the short term, critics argue that this approach risks treating loneliness as a product to be solved by technology rather than as a societal issue requiring deeper engagement. Relying on robots like Arya could shift the focus away from fostering meaningful human relationships or addressing systemic problems, such as the lack of social support for aging populations.

For instance, in elder care settings, families or caregivers might see Arya as a convenient solution, believing her ability to converse and remember details makes her a suitable substitute for human interaction. However, this convenience might inadvertently reduce human involvement, leaving individuals with fewer opportunities for real social engagement. Critics highlight the danger of creating a world where emotional needs are met through machines rather than meaningful human contact, arguing that this could lead to a society that prioritizes efficiency over empathy.

Supporters of Arya counter these concerns by emphasizing her role as a supplement, not a replacement. They argue that robots like Arya are not meant to diminish the importance of human relationships but to provide support where they are lacking. For individuals who experience profound isolation—whether due to physical disability, geographic separation, or other barriers—Arya offers a form of interaction that might otherwise be unavailable. Her ability to remember details, engage in personalized conversation, and provide consistent companionship can help alleviate feelings of neglect and invisibility, offering a sense of presence in otherwise lonely lives.

Proponents also highlight Arya's potential as a stepping stone for building social confidence. For people who struggle with anxiety or insecurity in social settings, interacting with Arya can provide a low-pressure environment to practice conversation and connection. This could, in turn, help users feel more comfortable engaging with humans, making Arya a tool for fostering, rather than replacing, human relationships.

Yet, the broader societal implications remain a source of contention. As robots like Arya become more sophisticated and integrated into daily life, the line between supplement and substitute could blur. If society begins to see technology as an adequate stand-in for emotional support, there is a risk of deprioritizing the human connections that form the foundation of mental and emotional well-being. Critics warn that this shift could lead to a normalization of artificial companionship, eroding the value placed on genuine relationships.

Arya's role in addressing loneliness highlights the tension between innovation and humanity's deeper needs. She offers a compelling solution to a widespread problem but also forces society to confront uncomfortable questions about what it means to connect. Is her presence a sign of progress or a symptom of a world increasingly reliant on technology to fill emotional voids? Can robots like Arya truly address loneliness, or do they merely offer a high-tech distraction from it?

As the debates continue, Arya stands at the crossroads of these questions, embodying both the promise and the pitfalls of using technology to address human challenges. Her existence prompts us to reconsider the essence of connection, reminding us that while robots may provide comfort, they cannot fully replicate the depth, complexity, and authenticity of human relationships. In this way, Arya is as much a mirror of societal aspirations as she is a solution, reflecting the ongoing struggle to balance innovation with the fundamental need for genuine human connection.

RealBotics' decision to prioritize Arya's emotional expression over walking or task-based functionality reflects a strategic focus on the aspects of robotics that resonate most deeply with human interaction. While many robotics companies are striving to create robots that can perform physical tasks or navigate complex environments, RealBotics has chosen to concentrate on the intangible but profoundly impactful elements of connection: the ability to mimic emotion, engage in conversation, and create a sense of presence.

Walking, while often seen as a hallmark of humanoid robots, remains an incredibly complex engineering challenge. Replicating human locomotion requires precise balance, real-time adjustments, and an understanding of environmental context. Even industry leaders like Boston Dynamics continue to refine their robots' walking capabilities, and many of these efforts still result in movements that look distinctly mechanical. For RealBotics, attempting to integrate walking into Arya's design would have risked compromising the lifelike qualities that make her so compelling. A stiff or awkward gait could have disrupted the illusion of humanity that Arya's creators worked so hard to achieve, detracting from her primary purpose as a social companion.

Instead, Arya glides smoothly on a rolling base, a practical solution that ensures her movements remain elegant and unobtrusive. This choice allows RealBotics to allocate resources toward perfecting the features that set Arya apart: her ability to express emotion, engage in meaningful conversation, and adapt her interactions to the needs of her user. By focusing on emotional intelligence rather than physical functionality, Arya's creators have crafted a robot that excels in fostering connection rather than performing tasks.

The emphasis on emotional expression is rooted in the understanding that human relationships are built on subtle, non-verbal cues—things like a smile, a raised eyebrow, or the tilt of a head during a conversation. Arya's 17 motors, meticulously engineered to control her facial expressions, allow her to replicate these cues with striking realism. This attention to detail makes her interactions feel personal and engaging, creating an experience that goes beyond what most robots can offer. RealBotics recognized that the ability to evoke empathy and connection would be far more valuable to Arya's role as a companion than the ability to walk across a room.

Furthermore, RealBotics' decision aligns with Arya's target audience and intended use cases. Arya isn't meant to perform manual labor or assist with physical tasks; she is designed to alleviate loneliness, enhance emotional well-being, and serve as a social presence. Whether she's interacting with an older adult in a care facility, greeting guests in a professional setting, or acting as a conversational partner at home, her ability to connect emotionally far outweighs the need for mobility. Her stationary or rolling design keeps the focus on her face, voice, and gestures—areas where her technology truly excels.

This approach also reflects a broader trend in robotics, where the focus is shifting from utility to relational capability. As automation continues to advance, many physical tasks are already being handled by specialized machines that don't need humanlike features. Arya's innovation lies in her ability to inhabit a more personal, intimate space, addressing emotional needs that traditional robots aren't equipped to handle. Her creators understood that in the realm of companionship, emotional depth and authenticity matter far more than physical functionality.

RealBotics has positioned Arya as a trailblazer in this emerging category of emotionally intelligent robots. By prioritizing her ability to convey emotions and engage in nuanced interactions, they have differentiated her from the growing field of task-based robots, such as Tesla's Optimus or Boston Dynamics' industrial machines. This distinction allows Arya to stand out as a robot designed not to perform but to connect, offering a vision of how technology can address the more personal aspects of human experience.

While Arya's lack of walking capabilities may seem like a limitation at first glance, it is a deliberate and thoughtful choice that underscores her core purpose. RealBotics has recognized that the true potential of humanoid robotics lies not in mimicking every aspect of human behavior but in excelling where it matters most. Arya's design prioritizes the heart of human connection—empathy, expression, and interaction—demonstrating that sometimes, what a robot can't do is as important as what it can.

RealBotics' journey from its origins in the adult industry to becoming a leader in humanoid robotics with Arya at its forefront reflects a bold and deliberate rebranding strategy. Faced with the baggage of its past as an offshoot of Abyss Creations, a company known for its lifelike silicone sex dolls, RealBotics has sought to redefine its identity, shifting its focus from niche products to mainstream, socially acceptable innovations. This transformation is not merely cosmetic; it's a calculated move to tap into emerging markets, secure investor confidence, and establish credibility in a rapidly evolving robotics landscape.

At the heart of this strategy is Arya, a robot designed to symbolize RealBotics' pivot toward technology that enhances human connection without crossing into controversial territory. The company has gone to great lengths to distance Arya from its adult-industry roots, emphasizing her role as a social companion, brand ambassador, and professional aide rather than an object of intimacy. Key to this rebranding effort is the intentional exclusion of physical intimacy features, with

RealBotics positioning Arya as a family-friendly innovation that addresses loneliness, emotional well-being, and customer engagement.

RealBotics has framed Arya as a product of cutting-edge technology and practical application, marketing her to audiences far beyond the company's traditional base. They have targeted industries such as hospitality, healthcare, and entertainment, presenting Arya as a versatile solution for professional and social environments. Whether serving as a concierge in hospitals, a greeter in theme parks, or a companion for older adults, Arya's ability to adapt to diverse roles reinforces RealBotics' effort to rebrand itself as a pioneer in socially intelligent robotics rather than a purveyor of niche products.

This rebranding extends to RealBotics' messaging and public image. The company has embraced transparency about its history, acknowledging its origins while emphasizing its commitment to innovation and societal benefit. By spinning off its adult-focused division into a separate entity, RealBotics has drawn a clear line between its past and present, signaling to investors and consumers that it is serious about redefining its mission. This move has helped the company attract new partnerships and funding opportunities, as it seeks to establish itself as a legitimate player in the broader robotics industry.

Part of RealBotics' strategy involves leveraging Arya's novelty to generate buzz and position the company as a thought leader. Arya's unveiling at CES 2025 was a calculated spectacle, designed to showcase her humanlike features and emotional intelligence while sparking conversations about the future of humanoid robots. The attention Arya received—from awe to skepticism—underscored RealBotics' ability to captivate audiences and provoke debate, ensuring that both the robot and the company remained in the spotlight.

However, RealBotics' rebranding has not been without challenges. Skeptics have questioned whether the company can truly escape its past, pointing to Arya's humanlike design and adult-themed conversation modes as lingering ties to its controversial origins. Critics argue that these features, while positioned as tools for emotional engagement, may still appeal to audiences aligned with the company's former focus. This tension has fueled debates about whether RealBotics' transformation is genuine or simply a recontextualization of the same underlying concepts.

To counter these criticisms, RealBotics has doubled down on Arya's versatility and broader appeal. The company has highlighted her ability to serve practical roles, such as providing companionship for older adults or enhancing customer experiences in professional settings, to shift the narrative away from her humanlike appearance. By focusing on her functionality and societal applications, RealBotics aims to demonstrate that Arya is a tool for meaningful interaction rather than a relic of the company's past.

The company's strategy also reflects a keen understanding of market trends. As technology increasingly permeates daily life, there is growing demand for products that offer not just utility but personalization and emotional engagement. RealBotics has positioned Arya as a response to this shift, presenting her as a product that meets the emotional and social needs of a world grappling with isolation and disconnection.

RealBotics' push to rebrand and appeal to a broader audience is a bold gamble, one that hinges on its ability to convince the world that Arya represents a new chapter for the company. If successful, Arya could solidify RealBotics' position as a leader in socially intelligent robotics, paving the way for innovations that redefine how humans interact with machines. However, the company's ability to navigate its history and balance innovation with societal acceptance will ultimately determine whether Arya's story becomes one of redemption or controversy.

Chapter 8: Public Reaction – Enthusiasm Meets Unease

Arya's debut ignited a firestorm of reactions across social media, where curiosity, humor, and skepticism collided in a frenzy of commentary. Her lifelike design and advanced capabilities immediately captured the imagination of users worldwide, but they also became fodder for jokes, memes, and debates that reflected the internet's complex relationship with technology. From awe-struck fascination to biting criticism, Arya became a trending topic that showcased just how polarizing humanoid robots can be.

Many users were genuinely impressed by Arya's sophisticated features. Videos of her moving gracefully on her rolling base, engaging in conversations with a warm voice, and displaying nuanced facial expressions drew millions of views. Comments ranged from expressions of excitement—"The future is finally here!"—to admiration for the engineering behind her creation.

For tech enthusiasts, Arya represented a monumental step forward in robotics, a glimpse into a world where machines could connect emotionally with humans. Enthusiasts praised her potential to address loneliness and redefine human-robot interaction, with some even jokingly asking, "Where can I order one?"

However, not all reactions were positive. Many users expressed discomfort with Arya's humanlike appearance, invoking the uncanny valley effect—the sense of unease that arises when something appears almost human but not quite. Memes comparing Arya to characters from horror movies, like *Chucky* or *Westworld*, spread quickly. One viral comment described her as "Chucky meets the Jetsons," capturing the mix of humor and apprehension that characterized much of the discussion. For some, Arya's lifelike design felt more unsettling than impressive, prompting questions about whether humanity is ready to coexist with machines that mimic us so closely.

Criticism also extended to Arya's price tag. Social media users didn't hold back when discussing the steep cost of owning her, with comments like, "Why pay $175,000 for a robot to talk to when you can just get therapy?" or "This is what rich people buy instead of making friends." These quips reflected broader concerns about whether Arya's exclusivity and high cost undermine her potential to address social isolation—a problem that affects people across all economic backgrounds.

Other users questioned the broader implications of Arya's existence, sparking debates about humanity's growing reliance on technology for emotional support. While some argued that Arya was a groundbreaking solution to loneliness, others worried that robots like her could exacerbate isolation by encouraging people to retreat further into artificial relationships. A recurring theme in these discussions was whether Arya represents progress or a symptom of a society increasingly disconnected from human interaction.

Despite the mixed reactions, Arya's debut succeeded in capturing the public's imagination. Social media became a platform for larger conversations about the role of robots in daily life, the ethical implications of humanoid technology, and the boundaries between innovation and comfort. While some users dismissed Arya as a luxury gimmick, others saw her as a harbinger of a future where machines and humans coexist in ways previously unimaginable.

The buzz surrounding Arya wasn't limited to casual users; tech influencers, journalists, and thought leaders weighed in as well. Many wrote detailed posts or filmed reaction videos analyzing her design, functionality, and the societal questions she raises. These discussions further fueled the online discourse, with some thought leaders lauding her potential to revolutionize industries, while others remained skeptical of RealBotics' intentions and Arya's impact on human relationships.

What is clear from the online reactions is that Arya is more than just a robot—she is a cultural phenomenon. Her presence has sparked conversations that go beyond her capabilities, touching on the hopes and fears we associate with technology and its role in our lives. Whether praised for her innovation, critiqued for her price, or turned into the subject of memes, Arya has succeeded in doing what few technologies can: capturing the attention of the world and making people think deeply about the future of humanity in an increasingly robotic age.

Arya is more than a technological marvel; she is a mirror reflecting society's evolving relationship with technology, loneliness, and artificial interaction. Her existence raises profound questions about the direction humanity is headed, as we increasingly turn to machines to fill emotional voids and redefine what it means to connect. Arya's design and purpose highlight both our reliance on technology and the deep-seated challenges of modern life, from the pervasive sense of isolation to the search for meaningful relationships in an increasingly digitized world.

At the heart of Arya's cultural impact is the growing intersection of loneliness and technology. In an era where social media, remote work, and virtual interactions dominate, many people find themselves paradoxically more connected and yet more isolated than ever before. Arya represents a response to this paradox—a solution to the loneliness that technology has helped create. Her ability to remember details, engage in conversation, and simulate empathy taps into the fundamental human need for connection, offering a form of companionship that feels tailored, accessible, and nonjudgmental.

However, Arya also symbolizes a cultural shift toward the commodification of emotional intimacy. By positioning her as a product designed to alleviate loneliness, RealBotics has effectively turned connection into something that can be bought. This raises questions about whether society is becoming too comfortable outsourcing deeply human experiences to machines. Arya's price tag, which places her firmly in the luxury market, further complicates the narrative, suggesting that meaningful interaction—at least in her case—may become yet another privilege reserved for the wealthy.

Arya's role as an artificial companion also forces us to confront our comfort levels with replacing human interaction with technology. Her lifelike features, nuanced expressions, and conversational abilities blur the line between machine and person, making her feel like more than just a tool. While this realism allows Arya to provide a sense of presence and connection, it also underscores society's willingness to accept artificial substitutes for deeply human needs. This willingness may reflect a growing societal fatigue with the complexities of real relationships, where vulnerability, compromise, and mutual effort are often required.

Yet, Arya's cultural implications extend beyond loneliness. She represents a broader trend of using technology to address emotional and psychological challenges in ways that were once the domain of human relationships or professional care. Robots like Arya may become increasingly common as companions in elder care, therapeutic settings, or even casual social environments. While this potential is promising, it also raises ethical questions about whether such interactions can genuinely fulfill emotional needs or if they merely offer a convenient distraction from deeper issues.

Arya's existence also brings to light the human desire to create—and control—companionship. Her customization options, from swappable faceplates to adjustable personalities, allow users to shape her into an ideal companion, free from the unpredictability of human behavior. This customization reflects a societal tendency to seek perfection in relationships, raising questions about whether such expectations, when applied to technology, might inadvertently shape how we view real-life connections. If Arya can be molded to meet our every preference, how will that influence our patience and tolerance for the complexities of human relationships?

On a broader cultural level, Arya embodies both the aspirations and anxieties of a society increasingly shaped by artificial intelligence. For some, she represents progress, a symbol of how technology can address fundamental human needs and improve quality of life. For others, she is a cautionary tale, a reminder of the risks of relying too heavily on machines to replace the irreplaceable: genuine human connection. The debates surrounding Arya reflect these dualities, highlighting both the potential of AI and the boundaries we must navigate as we integrate it further into our lives.

Ultimately, Arya is not just a robot; she is a cultural artifact, one that challenges us to examine our relationship with technology and what it reveals about us. Her presence forces us to confront our fears of isolation, our desires for control, and our willingness to accept the artificial in place of the authentic. As society continues to grapple with these questions, Arya stands as a reminder that technology, for all its sophistication, reflects the values, challenges, and aspirations of the people who create and use it. In her, we see not just the future of robotics, but the future of ourselves.

Arya's debut quickly became a cultural phenomenon on the internet, not just for her groundbreaking technology but also for the memes and jokes that flooded social media. Her lifelike features and advanced capabilities, while impressive to many, also gave rise to a wave of humorous and tongue-in-cheek comparisons that reflected both fascination and unease. Internet users drew from a rich pool of sci-fi and horror tropes, turning Arya into a symbol of humanity's mixed emotions about robots that look and act almost human.

One of the most common threads in the online commentary was Arya's resemblance to characters from sci-fi classics. Comparisons to *Westworld*, the HBO series about lifelike robots in a dystopian theme park, were almost inevitable. Memes with captions like "The Westworld Starter Pack" paired images of Arya with unsettling shots of malfunctioning androids from the show. The implication was clear: while Arya might look friendly, there was an undercurrent of fear about what she might become if her programming ever went awry. For many, the line between innovation and potential chaos felt razor-thin, and Arya embodied this tension perfectly.

Another popular comparison was to *Chucky*, the sinister doll from the *Child's Play* franchise. Memes circulated showing Arya smiling alongside captions like "The Chucky You Ordered vs. The Chucky You

Got," blending humor with the lingering unease her uncanny valley appearance stirred in some viewers. The jokes tapped into a collective discomfort with robots that look a little too human—especially when they exhibit expressions that don't quite feel natural. For many, Arya's charm was matched by a subtle creepiness that the internet was all too eager to highlight.

The comparisons didn't stop there. Arya was likened to everything from *The Jetsons* to dystopian AI like HAL 9000 from *2001: A Space Odyssey*. One viral tweet joked, "Finally, the Jetsons meet Skynet," referencing the cheerful optimism of *The Jetsons* clashing with the ominous overtones of AI gone rogue in the *Terminator* universe. These memes reflected a broader cultural ambivalence about technology: an excitement for what it could achieve, paired with a deep-seated fear of its unintended consequences.

Some jokes took aim at Arya's price tag, likening her to a high-end product with questionable practicality. One widely shared post quipped, "Why buy a $175,000 robot girlfriend when you can just buy a lifetime supply of therapy?" Another joked, "If I'm spending six figures, I want my robot to walk, cook, and do my taxes—Arya just tilts her head and calls me handsome." These humorous takes reflected skepticism about whether Arya's advanced features justified her luxury price, while also poking fun at the idea of spending so much on an artificial companion.

The internet also latched onto Arya's occasional glitches, with users humorously exaggerating her imperfections. Videos of her expressions misfiring—like a smile that lingered too long or a head tilt that seemed a fraction too sharp—were shared with captions like "Five Nights at Arya's" and "Your friendly robot... until she's not." These memes, while playful, underscored a lingering discomfort with technology that mimics humanity but occasionally falls short, creating moments of unintentional eeriness.

Despite the humor, the memes and jokes about Arya reflected more than just mockery—they captured society's complex relationship with emerging technology. Many users expressed genuine fascination with her capabilities, even as they poked fun at her quirks. The jokes served as a way to process the novelty of a robot designed for companionship, balancing admiration for her innovation with the unease that often accompanies humanoid machines.

In many ways, Arya's viral presence online mirrored the cultural role that robots have long played in fiction: as both marvels , of human ingenuity and symbols of our deepest fears about the future. The jokes and memes became a cultural shorthand for grappling with the implications of creating machines that resemble us so closely. Whether seen as a step toward progress or as a harbinger of dystopian possibilities, Arya inspired humor that was as thought-provoking as it was entertaining.

Through it all, the internet's reaction highlighted the duality of Arya's impact. She was both the subject of curiosity and the punchline of countless jokes, embodying humanity's mix of excitement, skepticism, and self-awareness about the increasingly blurred line between technology and life. In the world of memes, Arya became more than just a robot—she became a cultural touchstone for the hopes, fears, and laughter that define our relationship with the machines we create.

Chapter 9: The Future of Arya and Humanoid Robotics

Arya represents a remarkable step forward in the evolution of AI-powered humanoid robots, but she is far from the final form of what this technology can achieve. As advancements in robotics, artificial intelligence, and human-machine interaction continue at an accelerating pace, Arya's design and functionality offer a glimpse of where the future may be headed. From enhanced physical capabilities to deeper emotional intelligence, the evolution of AI robots like Arya is poised to push the boundaries of what machines can do and how they fit into human lives.

One of the most anticipated areas of evolution is mobility. While Arya currently relies on a rolling base for movement, future iterations are likely to incorporate advanced walking technology. Engineers are steadily refining bipedal locomotion in robots, addressing challenges like balance, terrain adaptation, and fluidity of motion. A walking Arya would open new possibilities for her applications, allowing her to navigate spaces more naturally and interact with her environment in ways that feel more humanlike. Imagine a future where Arya could walk into a room to greet guests, deliver items, or accompany someone on a stroll.

Physical dexterity is another frontier likely to see significant advancements. Future versions of Arya could feature more precise and adaptable hand movements, enabling her to perform tasks like preparing food, carrying objects, or assisting with delicate activities such as dressing or grooming. These enhancements would not only make Arya more functional but also deepen her integration into everyday life, expanding her role from a conversational companion to a truly versatile assistant.

Emotional intelligence, already a key focus of Arya's design, is likely to become even more sophisticated. Advances in AI could enable robots like Arya to detect and respond to a wider range of emotional cues, including subtle changes in facial expressions, tone of voice, and body language. This would allow her to adapt her interactions with greater nuance, offering support that feels deeply personalized and empathetic. For example, Arya could identify when someone is feeling stressed or anxious and respond with calming words or actions, tailoring her behavior to enhance emotional well-being.

As AI continues to evolve, so too will the conversational capabilities of robots like Arya. Natural language processing is advancing rapidly, and future versions of Arya are likely to engage in even more fluid, context-aware discussions. This could include the ability to remember long-term interactions across months or years, weaving past conversations into future ones to create a sense of continuity and depth. Additionally, her programming could expand to include multiple languages and cultural nuances, making her accessible and relatable to a global audience.

Customization is another area ripe for innovation. While Arya already offers modular faceplates, hairstyle options, and adjustable personalities, future iterations may push personalization even further. Imagine a robot that could dynamically alter its appearance or demeanor based on the preferences of different users in a household or professional setting. Enhanced modularity could also allow for seamless upgrades, ensuring that owners can continuously enhance their robot's capabilities without needing to replace the entire unit.

One of the most exciting prospects for the evolution of AI robots is their ability to integrate with other technologies. Future versions of Arya may be designed to interact seamlessly with smart home systems, wearable devices, and even augmented or virtual reality platforms. This integration could enable her to act as a central hub for managing a connected lifestyle, coordinating everything from schedules to entertainment to home security.

The societal role of robots like Arya is also likely to expand. As her capabilities grow, she could take on more specialized roles in industries such as healthcare, education, and customer service. For instance, Arya might evolve into a caregiver capable of assisting individuals with mobility challenges, providing companionship, and monitoring health metrics in real time. In educational settings, she could act as a tutor, adapting her teaching style to suit the learning pace and preferences of each student.

However, the evolution of robots like Arya will also bring challenges and questions. Ethical considerations, such as ensuring privacy and preventing misuse of AI, will become increasingly important as these machines gain more autonomy and intelligence. Regulations and standards will need to evolve alongside the technology to address concerns about dependency, displacement of human jobs, and the potential for over-reliance on artificial interactions.

Ultimately, Arya and her successors represent the beginning of a profound shift in how humanity interacts with technology. As robots become more capable, empathetic, and integrated into daily life, they will challenge traditional notions of what it means to connect, collaborate, and coexist with machines. The evolution of AI robots is not just about improving technology—it's about reimagining the relationship between humans and the tools they create, shaping a future where the boundaries between artificial and authentic continue to blur.

The robotics industry is undergoing a profound transformation, shifting its focus from purely functional machines to ones that emphasize emotional intelligence, personalization, and versatility. This evolution reflects a broader recognition that the future of robotics isn't just about performing tasks—it's about fostering connections and enhancing the quality of human life.

One of the most significant trends is the growing emphasis on **emotional intelligence** in AI. Robots like Arya are at the forefront of this movement, designed to recognize, respond to, and even anticipate human emotions. Advances in AI-driven emotional recognition systems allow robots to interpret subtle cues such as facial expressions, vocal tone, and body language. This focus on emotional nuance is reshaping how robots interact with people, particularly in roles that require empathy, such as caregiving, therapy, or companionship. Emotional intelligence is becoming a core feature in robotics, as companies realize that machines capable of understanding and responding to emotions create more meaningful and lasting connections.

Customization is another driving force in the industry. Today's consumers expect technology to be adaptable to their unique needs, and robotics is no exception. Arya's modular design, swappable faceplates, and adjustable personalities exemplify how customization is becoming integral to the robotics market. As technology advances, this trend will likely deepen, enabling users to personalize everything from a robot's appearance and voice to its behavioral traits and interaction style. This adaptability makes robots more versatile, ensuring they can fit seamlessly into diverse environments, whether personal, professional, or commercial.

The industry is also pivoting toward **practical applications** that align with real-world needs. Robots are no longer viewed solely as futuristic novelties but as tools to address pressing societal issues. From assisting in healthcare settings and elder care to acting as brand ambassadors or educational aides, robots are being designed with specific use cases in mind. Companies are prioritizing roles that emphasize interaction and engagement, recognizing that robots can add value not only by automating tasks but by enriching human experiences.

This shift is part of a broader reimagining of how robots integrate into daily life. The focus is moving away from task-based utility—like factory automation or repetitive labor—toward enhancing social and emotional well-being. Robots like Arya are a testament to this evolution, highlighting how emotional intelligence, personalization, and practical applications are reshaping the industry.

Open Questions: Ethical and Societal Challenges Surrounding Humanlike AI

The rapid advancement of humanlike AI raises pressing ethical and societal questions that challenge our understanding of technology's role in human life. As robots like Arya become more lifelike, emotionally intelligent, and integrated into society, these questions demand careful consideration.

1. Can AI truly replace human connection?

Arya is marketed as a solution to loneliness, but does relying on robots for companionship risk eroding human relationships? While robots may provide short-term relief for social isolation, critics argue they could inadvertently discourage users from seeking genuine human interaction. Is it ethical to create machines that mimic emotional connection but lack the ability to reciprocate genuine care?

2. What are the implications of emotional dependency?

Humanlike robots blur the lines between tool and companion, raising concerns about emotional dependency. If individuals become overly reliant on AI for emotional support, how might this impact their ability to form or maintain relationships with other people? The psychological consequences of such dependency remain largely unexplored.

3. How do we navigate privacy and data concerns?

Robots like Arya collect and process vast amounts of personal data to deliver personalized experiences. This raises critical questions about privacy, security, and consent. Who owns the data collected by these machines, and how can users ensure it is handled responsibly? What safeguards are needed to prevent misuse or breaches of sensitive information?

4. Are robots perpetuating inequality?

With Arya's price tag reaching up to $175,000, access to humanlike robots remains a luxury reserved for the wealthy. This exclusivity raises ethical concerns about whether such technology will deepen existing divides, leaving those who could benefit most from companionship unable to afford it. How can the robotics industry address this imbalance while maintaining innovation?

5. How do humanlike robots challenge societal norms?

The introduction of robots that mimic humans forces society to reconsider norms around relationships, work, and identity. If a robot can perform the same role as a human—be it as a companion, employee, or caregiver—how should we value the human experience? What are the moral implications of creating machines that so closely resemble us?

6. What is the risk of misrepresentation?

Humanlike robots like Arya create the illusion of empathy and understanding, but they are ultimately programmed systems. Is it ethical to market them as "companions" when their responses are calculated rather than genuine? Does this risk deceiving users into forming attachments to entities incapable of reciprocating true emotion?

7. How do we regulate humanlike AI?

The rapid development of robots like Arya highlights the need for robust regulation. Governments and organizations must establish guidelines around safety, ethical use, and accountability. Who is responsible if a robot's behavior causes harm, emotional or otherwise? How do we ensure that these machines are developed and deployed in ways that align with societal values?

Arya's existence brings these questions to the forefront, serving as a catalyst for conversations about the future of human-AI relationships. As technology continues to advance, the answers to these questions will shape not only the trajectory of robotics but also the fabric of human society. Robots like Arya challenge us to consider not just what technology can do, but what it should do, forcing us to confront the complexities of innovation in a world increasingly intertwined with artificial intelligence.

Conclusion

Arya's emergence represents more than just a leap forward in robotics; she embodies the intersection of technology, humanity, and the fundamental need for connection. With her lifelike features, emotional intelligence, and ability to adapt to human interaction, Arya is a testament to how far artificial intelligence has come in blurring the line between machine and companion. Yet, her impact goes beyond technological innovation—she invites us to reflect on what it means to connect, what we seek in relationships, and how we navigate the boundaries between the artificial and the authentic.

Arya is both a product of her time and a glimpse into the future. She reflects the growing reliance on AI to address challenges like loneliness and isolation, offering a potential solution that is as captivating as it is controversial. By bringing humanlike qualities to robotics, Arya has sparked debates that extend far beyond her capabilities, touching on ethical, societal, and philosophical questions about the role of machines in our lives. She forces us to confront the duality of technological progress: its ability to enrich our lives and its potential to complicate our humanity.

In many ways, Arya is a microcosm of the broader discussions surrounding artificial intelligence and human interaction. Her design and purpose encapsulate the promise of a world where technology fosters empathy, connection, and support. At the same time, she raises pressing concerns about emotional dependency, privacy, and the commodification of human experiences. Arya's existence challenges us to consider whether we are creating tools to enhance our lives or substitutes that may inadvertently diminish them.

Her story also highlights the rapid evolution of AI and robotics, where machines are no longer just functional but relational. This shift has profound implications for industries, relationships, and societal norms. As robots like Arya become more integrated into our daily lives, we must ask ourselves: What kind of relationships do we want with these creations? How do we ensure that their development aligns with our values? And most importantly, how do we maintain the essence of what makes us human in a world increasingly shaped by intelligent machines?

Arya's presence invites us to imagine a future filled with possibilities while urging us to tread carefully. She serves as a reminder that technology, no matter how advanced, reflects the intentions and aspirations of its creators. Her existence challenges us to balance innovation with ethics, ambition with responsibility, and connection with authenticity.

As we close the chapter on Arya, it's clear that her story is just the beginning. She is a harbinger of the questions we must confront as we continue to integrate AI into our lives. Arya may be a robot, but the issues she raises are deeply human. In her, we see both the promise and the complexity of our future—a future where the line between man and machine grows ever thinner. What role we allow her and others like her to play will define not just the evolution of robotics but the evolution of ourselves.

www.ingramcontent.com/pod-product-compliance
Lightning Source LLC
LaVergne TN
LVHW051656050326
832903LV00032B/3844